THE STORY OF THE CHICAGO CUBS

Published by Creative Education
P.O. Box 227, Mankato, Minnesota 56002
Creative Education is an imprint of The Creative Company

Design and production by Blue Design
Printed in the United States of America

Photographs by Associated Press (AP Photo/ho), Corbis (John Zich/Newsport), Getty Images (Lee Balterman//
Time Life Pictures, Bernstein Associates, Lisa Blumenfeld, W.E. Bowman/Lightfoot, Jonathan Daniel, John
Dominis//Time Life Pictures, Elsa, Fox Photos, Otto Greule Jr/Stringer, Adam Jones, VINCENT LAFORET/
AFP, National Baseball Hall of Fame Library/MLB Photos, Photo File, Photo File/MLB Photos, Rich Pilling/
MLB Photos, Mark Rucker/Transcendental Graphics, Chris Trotman, Ron Vesely/MLB Photos)

Library of Congress Cataloging-in-Publication Data

Omoth, Tyler.
The story of the Chicago Cubs / by Tyler Omoth.
p. cm. — (Baseball: the great American game)
Includes index.
ISBN-13: 978-1-58341-482-8
1. Chicago Cubs (Baseball team)—History—Juvenile literature. I. Title. II. Series.

GV875.C58O66 2007
796.357'640977311—dc22   2006029813

9 8 7 6 5 4 3 2

Cover: Shortstop Ernie Banks
Page 1: First baseman Cap Anson
Page 3: Pitcher Mark Prior

THE STORY OF THE
CHICAGO CUBS

by Tyler Omoth

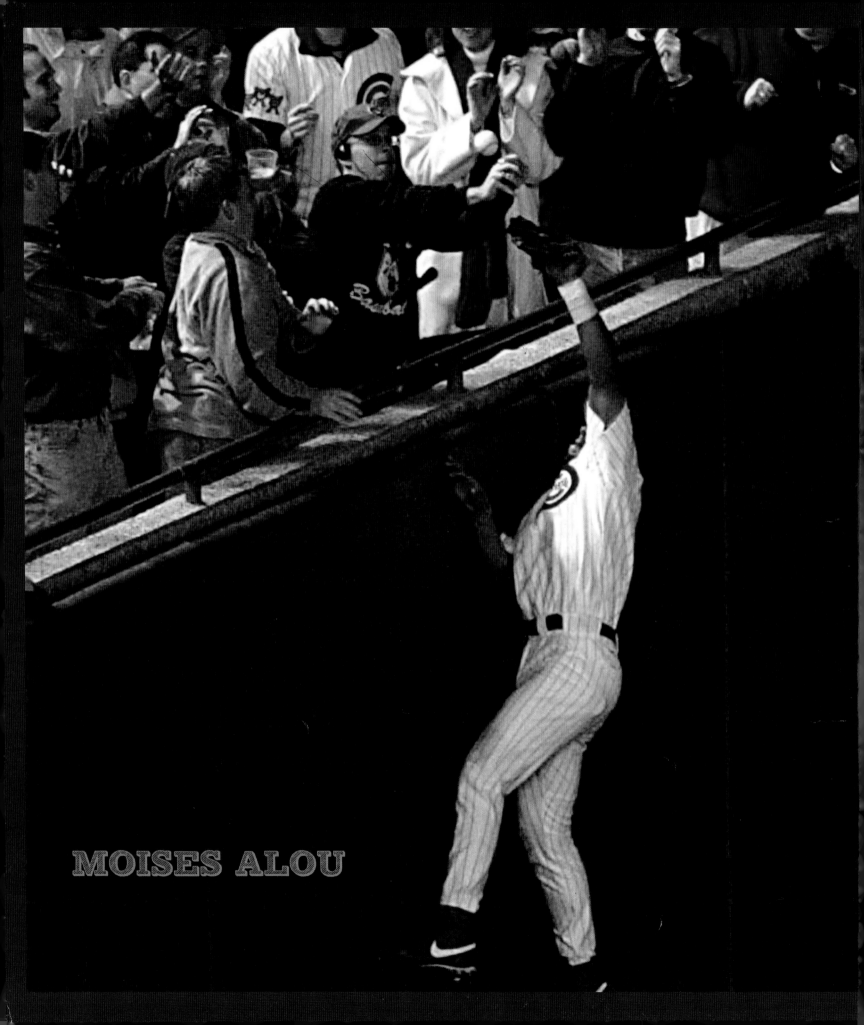
MOISES ALOU

THE STORY OF THE
Chicago Cubs

t had been 58 years since the Chicago Cubs had made it to the World Series when they found themselves on the brink of a "Fall Classic" in October 2003. Ahead 3–0 in Game 6 of the National League Championship Series, they were only five outs away as young starting pitcher Mark Prior looked to end the eighth inning. With the Wrigley Field crowd ready to erupt in celebration, Florida Marlins second baseman Luis Castillo flared a fly ball toward the left-field foul line. But just as Chicago left fielder Moises Alou reached up for the catch, a Cubs fan thoughtlessly reached for the souvenir and knocked the ball away from Alou's glove. Castillo promptly drew a walk, and the Marlins rallied to score eight runs and win the game and eventually the series. One of the worst collapses in baseball history became just another page in the story of a franchise  that is marked by, and adored for, its perennial frustration.

CUBS ORIGINS

**W**ith just under three million people, Chicago, Illinois, is the largest and most influential city in the Midwest. Resting on the banks of Lake Michigan, Chicago is commonly referred to as the "Windy City" because of the breezes that blow in from the lake. It has also been called the "City of Broad Shoulders" in honor of the hardworking, industrial nature of the people that call Chicago home. Although this bustling city boasts professional teams in every major American sport, including two Major League Baseball franchises, the Chicago Cubs are the oldest of them all.

When baseball's National League (NL) was founded in 1876, the Chicago White Stockings, who later be-

ADRIAN "CAP" ANSON – Anson was a baseball pioneer, the first player to get 3,000 career hits and a founder of spring training. He also holds the major-league record for fielding errors by a first baseman, due largely to the fact that players of his era did not use gloves.

CHICAGO

CHICAGO – In 1885, nine years after the White Stockings were formed, Chicago introduced the world's first skyscraper, a 10-story building. Today, the "Windy City" is home to two big-league baseball teams and America's tallest building, the Sears Tower.

came known as the Cubs, were one of the original teams. Led by player/manager A.G. Spalding and first baseman Adrian "Cap" Anson, the team was a success from the very beginning, winning the 1876 NL pennant. Spalding, however, retired two years later, and by 1879, Anson was the team's new manager. He went on to manage the club for 19 years, leading Chicago to five NL pennants by 1886. By the 1890s, the newly named Chicago Colts slipped low in the standings, where they'd remain until the turn of the century.

During the first 25 years of professional baseball, it was common for a team to go by several different names. The Chicago squad was known as the White Stockings, Colts, and even the Orphans. But when the club went through an obvious youth movement in 1902 under the leadership of new manager Frank Selee, a Chicago newspaper began to refer to the team as the "Cubs." By 1907, the team had adopted the title as its official name.

FRANK SELEE – It was under Selee's managerial watch that the Cubs went from perennial also-ran to NL contender. He was a quiet leader with a rare gift for spotting hidden talent in players and assembled Chicago's famous Tinker-Evers-Chance infield.

FRANK SELEE

1906 CUBS – The 1906 Cubs put together the best record in franchise history, going 116–36 to bring home the NL pennant. They assembled a stunning 1.75 team ERA and outscored their opponents 705–381 before losing the World Series in a stunning upset.

PITCHER · MORDECAI BROWN

When a boy grows up with a nickname like "Three Finger," his prospects of becoming a major-league pitcher are not too good. As a child, Mordecai Brown lost a finger in a farm machine accident. Later, while chasing a rabbit, he fell and broke his other fingers, leaving him with a bent middle finger, a paralyzed pinky, and a mere stump of an index finger. This odd combination, however, allowed him to get a grip on a baseball that provided excellent movement, much like the split-finger fastball thrown by pitchers today. Brown pitched 10 years for the Cubs, posting 6 consecutive seasons of 20 or more victories.

MORDECAI BROWN
PITCHER

CHICAGO
CUBS

STATS

Cubs seasons: 1904–12, 1916

Height: 5-10

Weight: 175

- **239–130 career record**

- **271 complete games**

- **2.06 career ERA**

- **Baseball Hall of Fame inductee (1949)**

The early years of the 1900s were golden ones for Cubs baseball. In 1907, another player/manager, first baseman Frank Chance, led the Cubs to their first World Series victory as they beat the Detroit Tigers and star outfielder Ty Cobb, winning four straight games after the teams tied in Game 1. The next year, the Cubs won the world championship again behind the pitching of Mordecai "Three Finger" Brown and the most famous double-play trio in history: shortstop Joe Tinker, second baseman Johnny Evers, and Chance. Franklin Pierce Adams, a writer for the *New York Evening Mail,* wrote of the Cubs' outstanding infield in poetic form, "Making a Giant hit into a double — / Words that are weighty with nothing but trouble: / Tinker to Evers to Chance."

Chicago infielders Joe Tinker (second from left), Johnny Evers (second from right), and Frank Chance (right).

TOO HOT OF A START

The National Association of Professional Baseball Players was founded in early 1871, with the Chicago White Stockings—an early name for the team that would later become the Cubs—as one of the league's inaugural teams. The White Stockings made a good showing in the young league by remaining contenders over much of that first summer, but adversity hit in early October. On October 8, 1871, the Great Chicago Fire (allegedly started when a cow kicked over a lantern in a barn) ravaged the city. The fire devastated more than 2,000 acres and, in the process, destroyed the White Stockings' ballpark, uniforms, and other equipment. The club was forced to finish its schedule playing in borrowed uniforms. Despite this setback, the White Stockings finished second in the standings in the National Association's inaugural year, trailing the Philadelphia Athletics by just two games. The havoc caused by the fire forced the team to drop out of the league while Chicago rebuilt from the ashes, but the White Stockings were revived in 1874. By 1876, the National Association gave way to the newly formed National League, and Chicago became a part of the league it still belongs to today.

BUILDING A TRADITION

T he second decade of the 20th century continued where the previous one had left off. The Cubs' power-hitting lineup punched Chicago's ticket to the World Series twice that decade, the first time in 1910. The team came up short that year, losing to the Philadelphia Athletics four games to one. The seasons that followed were mostly unspectacular but not without their highlights. In one game in June 1911, second baseman Heinie Zimmerman slugged his way into Cubs history with a team-record nine runs batted in (RBI) during a 20–2 rout of the Boston Red Sox. In 1918, the Cubs reached the World Series again but fell four games to two, this time to the Red Sox in a tight, low-scoring affair.

In 1916, the Cubs were purchased by Charles Weeghman, a former team owner in the Federal Baseball League, who moved the club to the north side of Chicago and into one of the most celebrated stadiums in baseball. The park was then known as Weeghman Park. In 1920, its name changed to Cubs Park, and in 1926, it was renamed once again in honor of new Cubs majority owner William Wrigley Jr.

Wrigley Field, known as "The Friendly Confines" because of its cozy dimensions and lively atmosphere, is still home to the Cubs today, making it

CATCHER · GABBY HARTNETT

Nicknamed "Gabby" by teammates during his rookie year, Charles Hartnett was actually quiet and polite—so much so that his fellow Cubs thought the nickname was perfect irony. Not only is he considered the best catcher in Cubs history, but he is commonly regarded as the best catcher in the NL before Cincinnati Reds great Johnny Bench put on the mask in 1967. A late bloomer, Hartnett hit his stride as he entered his 30s. From 1930 to 1937, he caught at least 100 games each year, and in 1939, he broke the big-league record of 1,727 career games behind the plate.

STATS

Cubs seasons: 1922–40

Height: 6-1

Weight: 195

- **.297 career BA**

- **236 career HR**

- **1935 NL MVP**

- **Baseball Hall of Fame inductee (1955)**

GABBY HARTNETT
CATCHER

CHICAGO
CUBS

A RUBBER-ARM DUEL

In baseball's early years, pitchers were expected to throw for more than just a few innings. Unlike today's game, there were no closers, and many starters stayed in to finish the games they began. On June 17, 1915, in a battle between the Brooklyn Dodgers and the Chicago Cubs, two pitchers went to extremes of endurance. Cubs hurler George "Zip" Zabel entered the game with just two outs in the first inning and pitched the remainder of the game. That may not seem like such an amazing feat, but this was no ordinary game; this game didn't finish until the 19th inning. Today, a pitcher completing a nine-inning game is a relative rarity, but that day, Zabel pitched 18 and 1/3 frames. What's more, the Dodgers' starting pitcher, Jeff Pfeffer, pitched the entire game too, scattering 15 hits while also going 18 and 1/3, only to take the loss. Zabel recorded the win as a throwing error by Dodgers second baseman George Cutshaw in the 19th inning allowed the Cubs to clinch a 4–3 victory. Ironically, Bert Humphries, the Cubs pitcher whom Zabel had replaced in the first, went on to lead the NL in complete games that season.

CUBS

Slugger Hack Wilson was almost cartoonishly muscular but showed surprising agility as a center fielder.

the second-oldest ballpark in Major League Baseball behind only Boston's Fenway Park. The ivy-covered outfield wall, classic marquee sign, and old-fashioned scoreboard make Wrigley Field a piece of baseball history that is adored by fans and players alike. Ernie Banks, a star shortstop for the Cubs in the 1950s and '60s, once praised its neighborhood atmosphere, saying, "Wrigley is like another home in the community. When you're in Wrigley, it's like you're visiting the family of all the people that live around here."

Despite their famous home, the Cubs managed only one first-place finish during the 1920s. The 1930s featured consistently good Cubs teams and many memorable moments. The team finished first in the NL in 1932, 1935, and 1938 but came up short in the World Series each year. Even though they were never quite able to win it all, the Cubs gave the Wrigley faithful plenty to remember during this era. In 1930, center fielder Hack Wilson put together

COMING HOME . . . AGAIN AND AGAIN

Throughout the Cubs' long history, the team has been involved in many historical and sometimes crazy games. On August 25, 1922, the Philadelphia Phillies came to town for what became the highest-scoring game in major-league history. Although the game lasted just the regular nine innings, the bats were scorching hot at Cubs Park that day as the Cubs edged the Phillies 26–23. No player had a better day at the plate than Cubs center fielder Cliff Heathcote, who went five-for-five with two doubles, five runs scored, and four RBI.

The Cubs came roaring right out of the box, scoring one run in the first inning and 10 runs in the second. Then, in the fourth inning, they added 14 runs to what looked like a monumental blowout. The Phillies weren't done yet, though. Having scored six runs up to that point, they added three more in the fifth inning, eight in the eighth, and then made the game really interesting by tacking on another six runs in the top of the ninth. By the final out, the teams had given the fans in attendance their money's worth, posting a total of 49 runs on 51 hits and 9 errors.

THE HOMER IN THE GLOAMIN'

After star catcher Gabby Hartnett was named the Cubs' new manager midway through the 1938 season, Chicago engaged in a race with the Pittsburgh Pirates for the NL pennant. On September 28, the Pirates came to Chicago with a half-game lead over the hometown Cubs. Because most parks did not have lights yet, games were played during the daytime. This game, a hard-fought battle, entered the ninth inning in a 5–5 tie. With two outs in the bottom of the ninth, the score remained tied as darkness began to settle over Wrigley Field. Realizing that the umpires would call the game on account of darkness after the inning, Hartnett stepped to the plate hoping to finish the contest quickly. Although he couldn't really see through the fading light, Gabby took a mighty swing where he hoped the pitch would be, and he connected, sending the ball screaming through the evening sky and over the fence. To this day, Hartnett's unlikely shot is known as "The Homer in the Gloamin'." That famous swing gave Chicago the lead over Pittsburgh in the pennant race, and the Cubs clinched the NL title three days later to reach their ninth World Series.

one of the most remarkable years ever at the plate, batting .356, clouting 56 home runs, and driving in 191 runs. In 1932, New York Yankees great Babe Ruth hit his famous "Called Shot" in Game 3 of the World Series versus the Cubs. And in the heat of the 1938 pennant race, catcher Gabby Hartnett hit a home run in near darkness to help the Cubs clinch the pennant—a shot that earned a place in baseball lore as "The Homer in the Gloamin'."

BIT BY THE GOAT

n 1945, the Cubs made it to the World Series once again, this time to be foiled by the Detroit Tigers in a seven-game series. For Chicago fans, the 1945 World Series would always be remembered for an even darker reason. A fan named Bill Sianis decided to attend Game 4 at Wrigley Field with his pet nanny goat, Senovia. Cubs officials would not allow Sianis to bring his goat into the park, claiming that the animal smelled bad and would disturb other fans. Angered by the refusal, Sianis uttered a curse that the Cubs would never again play in the World Series. To this day, fans still speak of the "Curse of the Billy Goat." After playing in 10 World Series from 1900 to 1945, the Cubs would not return to baseball's grand stage again.

The Cubs struggled at home in the 1945 World Series, losing three of the four games played at Wrigley Field.

The next few decades gave Cubs fans little to get excited about in terms of wins and championships. The team missed the playoffs year after year, even though its lineup featured a number of outstanding players. It was bittersweet to see great players play in Cubs uniforms because they were doomed, it seemed, to never see the postseason.

"Sweet Swingin'" Billy Williams, a dangerous hitter and dependable left fielder, and Ron Santo, a fiery third baseman, were among those who made their names in Cubs uniforms during the 1960s and '70s without ever experiencing the thrill of the playoffs. Slick-fielding shortstop Don Kessinger and talented pitchers Dick Ellsworth and Ken Holtzman won many games for the Cubs but likewise fell short of October baseball. Fan favorite Ernie Banks, known as "Mr. Cub," also played during this era, carving out a legendary career but never playing for a league or world championship. True to his upbeat nature, the Hall of Fame shortstop looked for the silver lining in the Cubs' drought, once remarking, "The only way to prove you're a good sport is to lose."

Another Cubs great, fireball-throwing pitcher Fergie Jenkins, also shone during the team's prolonged slump. Regarded as one of the greatest African American pitchers in the history of the game, Jenkins won at least 20 games a season for 6 years in a row (from 1967 to 1972). During each of those seasons, he managed to throw at least 20 complete games as well. Over a 10-year span,

FIRST BASEMAN · MARK GRACE

Mark Grace embodied the blue-collar spirit of Chicago. A line-drive hitter, Grace was often overshadowed by teammates such as outfielders Sammy Sosa and Andre Dawson, who consistently wowed crowds with picturesque home runs. Meanwhile, Grace quietly compiled more hits and more doubles than any other hitter in the major leagues between 1990 and 1999. Although the media spotlight often sought out the long-ball hitters, the Chicago faithful loved Grace for his consistency and spirited personality. His dry humor, sure fielding, and steady contributions in the middle of the Cubs' lineup made him a favorite in both the clubhouse and the stands.

MARK GRACE
FIRST BASEMAN

CHICAGO
CUBS

STATS

Cubs seasons: 1988–2000

Height: 6-2

Weight: 190

- **.303 career BA**

- **4-time Gold Glove winner**

- **3-time All-Star**

- **2,445 career hits**

SECOND BASEMAN · RYNE SANDBERG

Ryne Sandberg, known simply as "Ryno" to the baseball world, was a natural talent who played several positions before taking over second base for the Cubs in 1982, a spot he held for 15 years. Ryno was a quiet team leader who once put together a streak of 123 straight games without a fielding error. His career numbers placed him among the Cubs' all-time leaders in nearly every major batting category. After announcing his retirement in 1994, Sandberg came back to play two more years in 1996 and 1997, enabling him to pass Reds great Joe Morgan as the all-time home run leader among second basemen.

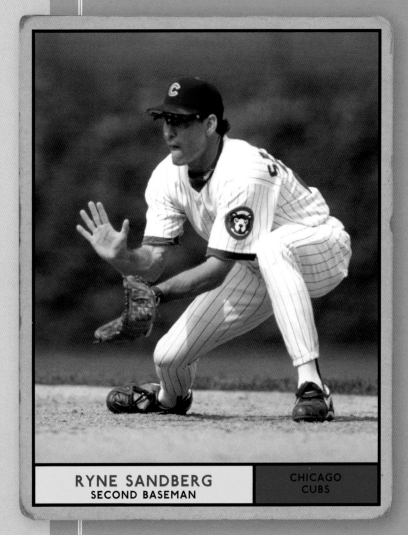

RYNE SANDBERG
SECOND BASEMAN

CHICAGO
CUBS

STATS

Cubs seasons: 1982–94, 1996–97

Height: 6-2

Weight: 180

- **1984 NL MVP**

- **10-time All-Star**

- **282 career HR**

- **Baseball Hall of Fame inductee (2005)**

Jenkins won 176 games for a team that never finished better than second in its league or division (the NL was split into Eastern and Western Divisions in 1969, with the Cubs placed in the East).

Banks retired in 1971, and by 1973, Jenkins was gone as well. Pitcher Bruce Sutter and outfielder Dave Kingman provided some highlights for the Cubs faithful during the late '70s, but by 1980, the Cubs had missed the playoffs for 35 consecutive seasons. Even the most ardent fans began to wonder if the Curse of the Billy Goat held some truth to it, but Chicago crowds assembled regardless of their team's record. The Cubs' home attendance numbers remained among baseball's best even as fan frustration set in.

In the early 1980s, Cubs fans celebrated some old heroes. In 1982, Jenkins came back to pitch two more years after spending eight seasons elsewhere and rang up his 3,000th career strikeout before hanging up his cleats in 1983. In 1982, the team honored Ernie Banks by making his number 14 the first to be retired by the organization.

The club also came under new leadership and found new stars during these years. The Wrigley family, which had owned the team since 1919, sold the Cubs to the Tribune Company (which owns the *Chicago Tribune* newspaper) for $20.5 million in 1981. And when the team added such talented young newcomers as outfielder Leon Durham and second baseman Ryne Sandberg, Chicago had good reason to hope the curse was about to end.

OH SO CLOSE . . . AGAIN

n 1984, behind the tremendous pitching of burly right-hander Rick Sutcliffe—who put up a 16–1 mark and won the Cy Young Award as the league's best pitcher—the Cubs won the NL East and made it to the playoffs for the first time since 1945. But Sutcliffe was not the only force behind this long-awaited success. Sandberg exploded onto the scene that season as well, batting .314 and stealing 32 bases. Durham, fellow outfielders Gary Matthews and Keith Moreland, and third baseman Ron Cey all put together solid seasons too to help the team finish 96–65 and meet the San Diego Padres in the NL Championship Series (NLCS). After winning the first two games of the series, the Cubs dropped three in a row to the Padres and lost the series, missing a berth in the World Series.

Although Sandberg continued to earn the adulation of fans in Chicago with his movie-star good looks, solid fielding, and powerful bat, the Cubs began to slide down the standings again. Then, in 1987, the team signed power-hitting right fielder Andre "The Hawk" Dawson. In his first season with the team, the Cubs went a mere 76–85, but The Hawk belted 49 home runs to win the NL Most Valuable Player (MVP) award. Even Sandberg was left in awe

RYNE SANDBERG – "Ryno" manned the second base position with machine-like precision, once going four seasons without making a single throwing error. From 1983 to 1991, he won nine straight Gold Glove awards as the league's best defensive second-sacker.

THIRD BASEMAN · RON SANTO

Some players wear their emotions on their sleeves, and Ron Santo was one of them. A feisty standout for the Cubs during the 1960s and early '70s, Santo was a great all-around third-sacker, winning five Gold Glove awards for his fielding prowess and hitting for both average and power. He also delighted Cubs fans by ritually clicking his heels in a celebratory dance each time the team won as the Cubs made a run at a pennant during the 1969 season. After his playing days ended, Santo embarked on a career in the radio booth as an analyst for the Cubs.

RON SANTO
THIRD BASEMAN

CHICAGO
CUBS

STATS

Cubs seasons: 1960–73

Height: 6-0

Weight: 190

- **5-time Gold Glove winner**
- **9-time All-Star**
- **342 career HR**
- **2,254 career hits**

LIGHTS AT WRIGLEY

The Cubs stood as a symbol of a baseball era gone by as they refused for many years to install lights at Wrigley Field. In fact, all Cubs home games were day games for the first 111 years of the club's history. Although it wasn't until 1988 that lights were added to Wrigley, that wasn't the first time that lights had been purchased for the stadium. Team president Philip K. Wrigley originally purchased a lighting system for Wrigley Field in 1942. However, after the bombing of Pearl Harbor, Wrigley donated the lights to the war effort. Then, as baseball's popularity skyrocketed in the decades following World War II, he decided that lights were not necessary at Wrigley. It wasn't until the club was sold to the Tribune Company in 1981 that the tradition of daytime-only games at Wrigley Field was pushed aside in favor of a more fan-friendly schedule, and lights were installed. Although public opinion was largely split on the issue, team ownership threatened to move the Cubs if night games could not be a part of the schedule. The very first game under lights at Wrigley Field was played on August 9, 1988, as the Cubs defeated the New York Mets 6–4.

CUBS

ANDRE DAWSON

Andre Dawson was so feared that he
was intentionally walked a big-league
record five times in one 1990 game.

of Dawson's amazing season, later saying, "I watched him win an MVP for a last-placed team in 1987, and it was the most unbelievable thing I've ever seen in baseball."

By 1989, Chicago was again poised to make a playoff run. Along with Dawson and Sandberg, the Cubs featured emerging talents such as strong-armed shortstop Shawon Dunston and line-drive-hitting outfielder Jerome Walton, who won the NL Rookie of the Year award that season. The 1989 Cubs went 93–69 and won the NL East again. But, once again, they lost in the

SHAWON DUNSTON

SHAWON DUNSTON – Although his free-swinging approach made him a streaky hitter, Dunston paired with Ryne Sandberg to form a marvelous double-play duo. The teammates played together in the All-Star Game in both 1988 and 1990.

NLCS, this time to the San Francisco Giants in five hard-fought games. Mark Grace, a first baseman in his second year with the team, made headlines by going 11-for-17 with 8 RBI in the NLCS, providing a bright side to an otherwise disappointing outcome.

After the excitement of the 1980s, the '90s turned out to be a decade mostly of mediocrity for the Cubs. Dawson left in 1992 but was replaced by a young slugger named Sammy Sosa. The brawny right fielder consistently drove in 100 or more runs each season, but it was his jovial personality and ability to hit mammoth home runs that made him a Wrigley fan favorite. A native of the Dominican Republic, Sosa combined the youthful enthusiasm of Ernie Banks with the raw power of Hack Wilson, becoming one of the most exciting players ever to wear Cubs blue.

Still, it wasn't until 1998 that the Cubs came back on the scene as a playoff team and a point of national interest. The club's pitching rotation that season featured the powerful arm of rookie Kerry Wood. Wood threw a fastball that consistently topped 95 miles per hour, and he took the league by storm despite being just 20 years old. In only his fifth start, he threw a one-hitter against the Houston Astros while striking out 20 batters, a staggering feat that tied legendary strikeout pitcher Nolan Ryan's big-league record. Wood went on to accumulate a 13–6 record, although a tender elbow sidelined him toward the end of the Cubs' run to the postseason.

SHORTSTOP · ERNIE BANKS

In the long and colorful history of the Chicago Cubs, perhaps no player was as beloved as Ernie "Mr. Cub" Banks. Known for his constantly cheerful disposition, Banks enjoyed the game so much that his favorite phrase, rain or shine, was "Let's play two!" When he joined the team in 1953, Banks became the Cubs' first black player. Although he actually played more games at first base than any other position, Banks will always be remembered as an energetic shortstop who hit for far more power than his lean frame suggested was possible. When he retired in 1971, his number (14) became the first retired by the Cubs.

STATS

Cubs seasons: 1953–71

Height: 6-1

Weight: 180

- 512 career HR

- 2-time NL MVP

- 11-time All-Star

- Baseball Hall of Fame inductee (1977)

ERNIE BANKS
SHORTSTOP

CHICAGO CUBS

KERRY WOOD – Wood's Cubs career was an up-and-down ride. After an electrifying rookie debut in 1998, he missed the 1999 season recovering from elbow surgery. He posted double-digit wins in 2001, 2002, and 2003 before struggling with injuries again.

CUBS

While Wood was fanning opposing batters, Sosa was captivating the sports world as he engaged brawny St. Louis Cardinals first baseman Mark McGwire in a two-man contest to beat New York Yankees outfielder Roger Maris's single-season home run mark of 61. The two sluggers were neck and neck for the majority of the season in a competition that thrilled fans around the country and led to a resurgence in the popularity of the national pastime. In the end, McGwire was the first to surpass the record, finishing with a whopping 70 home runs for the season, with Sosa clubbing a grand total of 66 homers.

Along with timely team hitting and great pitching from Wood and 19-game winner Kevin Tapani, Sosa's heroics were enough to give the Cubs a 90–73 record and a playoff berth as a Wild Card team after beating the Giants in a special one-game playoff. Unfortunately, the Cubs came up short once again on the postseason stage, losing to the Atlanta Braves in three straight games in the NL Division Series (NLDS).

After making his 2001 Cubs debut at 20 years old, 6-foot-5 hurler Carlos Zambrano quickly became a star.

CARLOS ZAMBRANO

A MISSED OPPORTUNITY

The new millennium was welcomed with another sub-par season on Chicago's north side, but the Cubs turned things back around in 2001. Putting together an 88–74 record, the team missed the playoffs but played winning baseball, thanks largely to great pitching. Right-handed starter Jon Lieber earned a trip to the 2001 All-Star Game by winning 20 games, and Wood continued to baffle hitters, striking out 217. In 2002, young pitcher Mark Prior—the second overall pick in baseball's 2001 draft—made his big-league debut, beginning what fans hoped would be a long and productive career.

The Cubs returned to the playoffs in 2003, a postseason that would prove unforgettable for all the wrong reasons in Chicago. Under the leadership of new manager Dusty Baker, the team posted another 88–74 mark but this time found itself on top of the NL Central Division. Once again, Chicago faced the Atlanta Braves in the NLDS. This time, however, the Cubs were up to the task, beating the Braves three games to two and moving on to the NLCS. After dropping Game 1 to the Florida Marlins, the Cubs trounced the Marlins 12–3 in Game 2 to even the series. The Cubs won again in Game 3 in 11 innings. Then, after the teams split the next two games, the series went back

LEFT FIELDER · BILLY WILLIAMS

"Sweet Swingin'" Billy Williams was a constant presence in left field for the Cubs from the early 1960s to the mid-1970s, setting an NL record with 1,117 consecutive games played. Williams is considered by many people to be one of the most overlooked stars of his time. He lacked the flash of teammates Ron Santo or Ernie Banks, yet he consistently put up spectacular hitting statistics, stringing together 13 straight seasons of at least 20 home runs and 84 RBI. Williams never got the chance to play in a World Series, but his stellar career earned him a spot in the Baseball Hall of Fame.

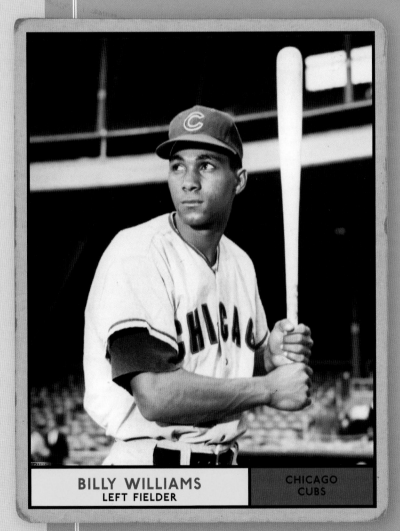

BILLY WILLIAMS
LEFT FIELDER

CHICAGO
CUBS

STATS

Cubs seasons: 1959–74

Height: 6-1

Weight: 175

- **1961 NL Rookie of the Year**

- **6-time All-Star**

- **.290 career BA**

- **Baseball Hall of Fame inductee (1987)**

CENTER FIELDER · HACK WILSON

Standing only 5-foot-6, Lewis Wilson did not look the part of a major-league baseball player. His nickname, "Hack," is said to have its origins in his resemblance to a professional wrestler named George Hackenschmidt. Wilson and his Cubs career were both short and intense. With a free-swinging style, the muscular outfielder terrorized pitchers for six seasons in a Chicago uniform. In 1930, he put together one of the best offensive seasons the game has ever seen, hitting .356 with 56 home runs and 191 RBI. That incredible RBI total remains a major-league record.

HACK WILSON
CENTER FIELDER

CHICAGO
CUBS

STATS

Cubs seasons: 1926–31

Height: 5-6

Weight: 190

• **.307 career BA**

• **4-time NL leader in HR**

• **1,063 career RBI**

• **Baseball Hall of Fame inductee (1979)**

THE VOICE OF A LEGEND

Perhaps nothing is more synonymous with a Chicago Cubs game than the image of Harry Caray leaning out from his television broadcast booth and waving his microphone at the crowd as he led it in a rendition of "Take Me Out to the Ballgame" during the seventh-inning stretch at Wrigley Field. Caray began his career as a broadcaster for the St. Louis Cardinals in 1945 but became a legend as the voice of the Cubs from 1982 to 1997. Known for his jovial spirit, Caray embodied the attitude of the "bleacher bums" in Wrigley, those blue-collar, fun-loving fans who made the outfield seats a constant good-natured party. That spirit earned him the nickname, "The Mayor of Rush Street," a reference to a particularly festive part of Chicago. Caray's broadcasting mannerisms have been widely parodied and copied by broadcasters and comedians alike. A particular favorite of fans was his tendency to mispronounce players' names and sometimes even get them backwards! His trademark exclamation, "Holy cow!" put an exclamation point on many great and not-so-great plays by the Cubs during his 16 years as Chicago broadcaster. And when the home team would come out on top, fans couldn't wait to hear his favorite words: "Cubs win! Cubs win!"

CUBS

[41]

to Wrigley Field with the Cubs up three games to two and needing only one victory with two games remaining.

It looked as if Chicago was going back to the World Series for the first time since 1945 as the Cubs found themselves up 3–0 with one out in the eighth inning. Then disaster struck. Marlins second baseman Luis Castillo popped a foul ball toward the left-field stands that would almost certainly have been caught had a fan not interfered. Then Marlins right fielder Miguel Cabrera hit a grounder for what should have been an inning-ending double play, but normally sure-handed Cubs shortstop Alex Gonzalez booted the ball, allowing the inning to continue. Before the Cubs could get out of the nightmarish inning, the Marlins had scored eight runs and taken an insurmountable lead. Florida went on to win Game 7 by a 9–6 score. "It has nothing to do with the curse," Baker said of the instantly infamous eighth inning. "It has to do with fan interference and a very uncharacteristic error."

The heartbreaking loss seemed to bring more misfortune on the Cubs, as young aces Wood and Prior struggled with injuries in the following seasons and the Cubs fell in the standings. Still, Chicago kept up its efforts to capture that long-elusive pennant. In 2004, the team signed slugging

Fans counted on Derrek Lee, who signed a $65-million contract in 2006, to carry the Cubs back into the playoffs.

DERREK LEE

ARAMIS RAMIREZ

RIGHT FIELDER · SAMMY SOSA

Sammy Sosa's career in a Cubs uniform was a roller coaster ride of emotion for both the right fielder and the Chicago faithful. Beginning in 1995, "Slammin' Sammy" posted 9 consecutive seasons with more than 30 home runs and 100 RBI. He went on to become one of the most prolific home run hitters of all time, and in 1998, he and St. Louis Cardinals first baseman Mark McGwire engaged in an unforgettable race to eclipse baseball's hallowed single-season home run record. Relations between the slugger and Cubs officials soured in 2004, leading to his departure.

SAMMY SOSA
RIGHT FIELDER

CHICAGO
CUBS

STATS

Cubs seasons: 1992–2004

Height: 6-0

Weight: 220

- **588 career HR**
- **1998 NL MVP**
- **7-time All-Star**
- **2-time NL leader in RBI**

MANAGER · FRANK CHANCE

Frank Chance was a solid-hitting first baseman for the Cubs from 1898 to 1912. In the middle of the 1905 season, Chance took over as player/manager for the team at the tender age of 27. During his tenure as manager, the Cubs never fell below third place in the NL and four times finished with more than 100 victories in a season. Nicknamed "The Peerless Leader," Chance led the Cubs to pennants in 1906, 1907, 1908, and 1910. He managed the way he played, with a hard-nosed, no-nonsense style that players respected. Under their Peerless Leader, the Cubs won the World Series in 1907 and 1908.

FRANK CHANCE
MANAGER

CHICAGO
CUBS

STATS

Cubs seasons as manager: 1905–12

Height: 6-0

Weight: 190

Managerial Record: 946–648

World Series Championships: 1907, 1908

first baseman Derrek Lee and saw him blossom into one of the game's elite hitters; in 2005, he batted .335 with 46 home runs and 107 RBI. The Cubs also added veteran leadership by bringing back future Hall of Fame pitcher Greg Maddux, who had spent seven fine seasons with the club in the late 1980s and early '90s.

Although the Cubs ended the 2006 season 66–96 and at the bottom of the NL Central, the emergence of new talents such as pitcher Carlos Zambrano and hard-hitting third baseman Aramis Ramirez gave Chicago's "bleacher bums" hope. Cubs management gave fans two more big reasons for hope in the off-season by signing Alfonso Soriano, an outfielder with a rare combination of blazing speed and home run power, and hiring longtime manager Lou Piniella as the team's new leader. "The kids [players] have a feeling a lot of good things can happen in Chicago this year," said Piniella before the 2007 season.

Few teams in any sport can boast the kind of history and tradition the Chicago Cubs have built. And even fewer can lay claim to the kind of loyalty and affection that the Cubs have received from their many fans over the years. Although no team has gone longer without a World Series than the Cubs, each Chicago spring is greeted with hope and the possibility that this is the year the "Cubbies" will finally win it all. The Windy City is sure to be a noisy place the day the Cubs break the Curse of the Billy Goat and capture another world championship.